great Cotton Tops

LION BRAND® 24/7 COTTON® YARN

Offering wonderful comfort and style around the clock, 24/7 Cotton® Yarn is a great choice for the tops in this design collection. The mercerization process of this worsted-weight, 100 percent natural fiber yarn creates incredible color and sheen that will last through multiple wash cycles. Its 24 colors are perfect for making fashion garments, home décor, bath and kitchen accessories, and items for babies and children.

I0866882

About Lion Brand® Yarn Company

Lion Brand® Yarn Company is a 5th generation, family-owned and operated business, and a beloved American brand since 1878. The company is devoted to inspiring and educating knitters and crocheters with yarns, patterns, how-tos, and ideas that elevate their yarn crafting experience.

LEISURE ARTS, INC.
Maumelle, Arkansas

beach Coverup

EASY +

SIZES

XS/S{M/L-1X/3X}

Finished Bust:

42{50-58}"/106.5{127-147.5} cm

Finished Length:

27{28-29}"/68.5{71-73.5} cm

Note: Pattern is written for smallest size with changes for larger sizes in parentheses. When only one number is given, it applies to all sizes. To follow pattern more easily, circle all numbers pertaining to your size before beginning.

SHOPPING LIST

Yarn (Medium Weight) MEDIUM 4

LION BRAND® 24/7 COTTON®
(Art. #761)

- ☐ #100 White - 3{4-5} balls (A)
- ☐ #110 Navy - 2{3-3} balls (B)
- ☐ #172 Grass - 1{2-2} ball(s) (C)

Crochet Hook

LION BRAND® crochet hook

- ☐ Size F-5 (3.75 mm)
  or size needed for gauge

Additional Supplies

- ☐ LION BRAND® stitch markers
- ☐ LION BRAND® large-eyed blunt needle

GAUGE

3 pattern reps + 7½ rows = about 4" (10 cm) in pattern of Back Rows 1-6.

Note: In Rows 1, 2, 5, and 6, one pattern rep consists of 3 (ch 1, dc) groups. In Row 3 one pattern rep consists of one diamond and the following dc.

BE SURE TO CHECK YOUR GAUGE.

STITCH GUIDE

DIAMOND

Dc in indicated ch-sp, ch 3, work 3 dc around the post of the dc just made.

NOTES

1. Back and Front are worked separately.
2. Both pieces are worked the same from the lower edge upwards. Chains are joined to sides of each piece at underarms for sleeves.
3. Back and Front are crocheted together.
4. An edging is worked along lower edges.
5. To change yarn color, work last st of old color to last yarn over. Yarn over with new color and draw through all loops on hook to complete st. Proceed with new color. Fasten off old color.

BACK

With B, ch 100{118-136}.

Row 1 (RS): Dc in 6th ch from hook (5 skipped ch count as 1 base ch, first dc and ch-1), *ch 1, sk next ch, dc in next ch; rep from * across – you will have 49{58-67} dc and 48{57-66} ch-1 sps in this row (for 16{19-22} pattern reps).

Row 2: Ch 4 (counts as dc, ch 1), turn, sk next ch-1 sp, dc in next dc, *ch 1, sk next ch-1 sp, dc in next dc; rep from * to beg ch-sp, ch 1, dc in 4th ch of beg ch.

Row 3: Ch 3 (counts as dc), turn, sk first ch-1 sp, diamond in next ch-1 sp, *sk next ch-1 sp, dc in next dc, sk next ch-1 sp, diamond in next ch-1 sp; rep from * to beg ch-sp, dc in 3rd ch of beg ch-4 – 16{19-22} diamonds.

Row 4: Ch 5 (counts as dc, ch 2), turn, sc in top of ch-3 of next diamond, *ch 2, dc in next dc, ch 2, sc in top of ch-3 of next diamond; rep from * to beg ch-3, ch 2, dc in top of beg ch-3 – 2 dc, 16{19-22} sc, and 32{38-44} ch-2 sps.

Row 5: Ch 4 (counts as dc, ch 1), turn, dc in first ch-2 sp, *ch 1, sk next sc, dc in next ch-2 sp, ch 1, dc in next dc, ch 1, dc in next ch-2 sp; rep from * to last sc, ch 1, sk last sc, dc in beg ch-sp, ch 1, dc in 3rd ch of beg ch-5 and change to C.

Row 6: With C, ch 4 (counts as dc, ch 1), turn, sk first ch-1 sp, dc in next dc, *ch 1, sk next ch-1 sp, dc in next dc; rep from * to beg ch-sp, ch 1, dc in 3rd ch of beg ch-4.

Rows 7-30: Rep Rows 3-6 changing color as in following color sequence: Work 1 more row with C, 2 rows with B, 4 rows with C, 2 rows with B, 2 rows with C, 4 rows with B, 2 rows with A, 2 rows with B, 5 rows with A.

Rows 31-34: With A, rep Row 6. Do NOT fasten off.

Beg Sleeves

Drop loop from hook and enlarge it so that it does not unravel. With a separate length of A, ch 36 for underarm ch, join ch-36 with sl st in 3rd ch of beg ch-4 of Row 34. Fasten off.

Return dropped loop to hook.

Row 35 (RS): With A, ch 39 for underarm ch, turn, dc in 6th ch from hook (5 skipped ch count as 1 base ch, first dc and ch-1), (ch 1, sk next ch, dc in next ch) 16 times, ch 1, sk next ch, dc in next dc, *ch 1, sk next ch-1 sp, dc in next dc; rep from * to beg ch-sp, ch 1, dc in 3rd ch of beg ch-4; working along underarm ch, (ch 1, sk next ch, dc in next ch) 18 times – 85{94-103} dc and 84{93-102} ch-1 sps (28{31-34} pattern reps).

Row 36: With A, ch 4 (counts as dc, ch 1), turn, sk first ch-1 sp, dc in next dc, *ch 1, sk next ch-1 sp, dc in next dc; rep from * to beg ch-sp, ch 1, dc in 5th ch of beg ch.

Rows 37-44{46-48}: With A, ch 4 (counts as dc, ch 1), turn, sk first ch-1 sp, dc in next dc, *ch 1, sk next ch-1 sp, dc in next dc; rep from * to beg ch-sp, ch 1, dc in 3rd ch of beg ch-4.

Next 3 Rows: With A, rep Rows 3-5 and change to B in last st of last row.

Next Row: With B, rep Row 6.

Next 3 Rows: With B, rep Rows 3-5. Fasten off.

FRONT

Make same as Back to last row. Place markers on Back in dc immediately above the dc following the 5th{5th-6th} diamond, 10th{11th-12th} diamond, 18th{20th-22nd} diamond, 23rd{26th-28th} diamond, and in last dc.

Last Row (Joining Row): Hold WS of Front and Back together with sts matching. Turn to work from RS of Front, ch 3 (counts as dc), sl st in first dc of Back, sc in next ch-1 sp of Back; *working in Front sts only, dc in next ch-2 sp, ch 1, sk next sc, dc in next ch-2 sp, (ch 1, dc in next dc, ch 1, dc in next ch-2 sp, ch 1, sk next sc, dc in next ch-2 sp) to next marker on Back **, sc in ch-1 sp of Back before marked dc, dc in next dc of Front, sc in ch-1 sp of Back after marked dc, remove marker; rep from * across ending last rep at **, sc in beg ch-sp of Back, dc in 3rd ch of beg ch-5 of Front, sl st in 3rd ch of beg ch of Back.
Fasten off.

FINISHING

Sew sleeve and side seams, leaving about 7" (18 cm) unsewn on each side above lower edge for side slits.

Lower Edging

From RS, join C with a sc anywhere in lower edge, *ch 1, sc in edge; rep from * working as evenly spaced as possible all the way along lower edge including edges of side slits and working (sc, ch 1, sc) in each corner; join with sl st in first sc. Fasten off.

Weave in ends.

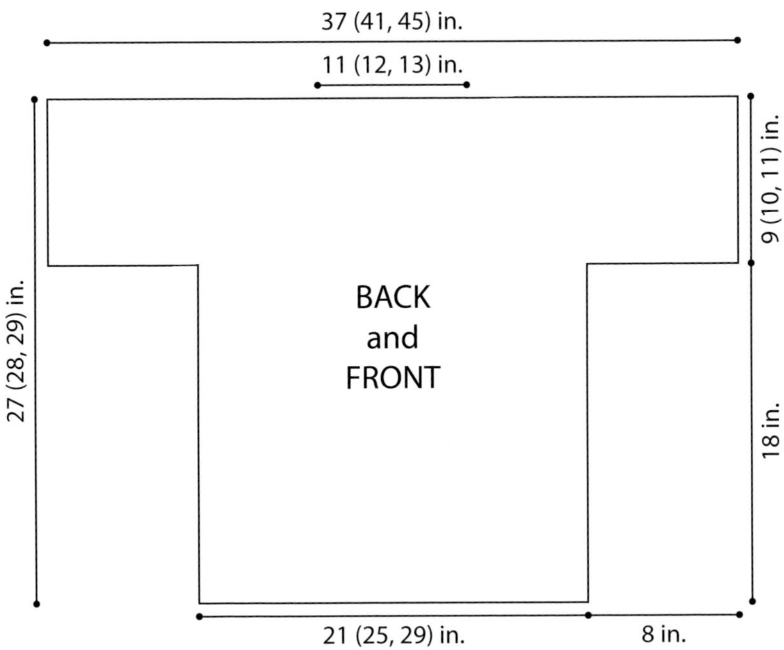

flower Lace Tunic

EASY +

SIZES

XS/S{M/L-1X/3X}

Finished Bust:

38{46-54}"/96.5{117-137} cm), unstretched – Tunic is very stretchy

Finished Length:

29{30-30½}"/73.5{76-77.5} cm

Note: Pattern is written for smallest size with changes for larger sizes in parentheses. When only one number is given, it applies to all sizes. To follow pattern more easily, circle all numbers pertaining to your size before beginning.

SHOPPING LIST

Yarn (Medium Weight) MEDIUM 4

LION BRAND® 24/7 COTTON® (Art. #761)

☐ #100 White - 7{8-10} balls

Crochet Hook

LION BRAND® crochet hook

☐ Size F-5 (3.75 mm) **or** size needed for gauge

Additional Supply

☐ LION BRAND® large-eyed blunt needle

GAUGE

1 Flower Square = about 5" (12.5 cm) across.

BE SURE TO CHECK YOUR GAUGE.

STITCH GUIDE

2 DOUBLE CROCHET CLUSTER (abbreviated 2-dc Cl)

Yarn over, insert hook in indicated st and draw up a loop, yarn over and draw through 2 loops on hook (2 loops rem on hook), yarn over, insert hook in *same* st and draw up a loop, yarn over and draw through 2 loops on hook, yarn over and draw through all 3 loops on hook.

3 DOUBLE CROCHET CLUSTER (abbreviated 3-dc Cl)

Yarn over, insert hook in indicated st, yarn over and draw up a loop, yarn over and draw through 2 loops on hook (2 loops rem on hook), (yarn over, insert hook in *same* st, yarn over and draw up a loop, yarn over and draw through 2 loops on hook) twice; yarn over and draw through all 4 loops on hook.

CHAIN-4 JOIN (abbreviated ch-4 join)

Ch 2, sl st in corresponding ch-4 sp of previous Flower Square, ch 2.

PATTERN STITCH

Lace Pattern

Row 1 (RS): Ch 1, turn, sc in first dc, ch 2, sk first ch-2 sp, 2-dc Cl in next sc, *ch 2, sc in next ch-5 sp, ch 2, 2-dc Cl in next sc; rep from * to beg ch-5, ch 2, sc in 3rd ch of beg ch-5.

Row 2: Ch 5 (counts as dc, ch 2), turn, sc in next Cl, *ch 5, sk next sc, sc in next Cl; rep from * to last ch-2 sp, ch 2, sk last ch-2 sp, dc in first sc.

Rep Rows 1 and 2 for Lace pattern.

NOTES

1. Tunic Front and Back are worked separately, then seamed. Sleeves are worked directly onto the sides of the seamed Front and Back.
2. A grid of Flower Squares is made for center of Front and Back. Lace pattern Neck, Sides, and Lower Edging are added to Flower Square center.
3. Flower Squares are worked in joined rnds with RS always facing. After the first Flower Square is made, following Flower Squares are joined to the previous Flower Squares.

BACK

First Flower Square

Ch 5; join with sl st in first ch to form a ring.

Rnd 1 (RS): Ch 1, work 12 sc in ring; join with sl st in first sc – you will have 12 sc in this rnd.

Rnd 2: *Ch 11, sl st in next sc; rep from * around – 12 sl sts and 12 ch-11 sps.

Rnd 3: Sl st in first 5 ch of first ch-11 sp, (sl st, ch 1, sc) in next ch of same ch-11 sp, ch 4, sc in 6th ch of next ch-11 sp, ch 4, (3-dc Cl, ch 4, 3-dc Cl) in next ch-11 sp (corner made), *(ch 4, sc in 6th ch of next ch-11 sp) twice, ch 4, (3-dc Cl, ch 4, 3-dc Cl) in next ch-11 sp; rep from * 2 more times, ch 4; join with sl st in first sc – 4 (3-dc Cl, ch 4, 3-dc Cl) corners, 12 ch-4 sps, and 8 sc.

Rnd 4: Sl st in first 2 ch of first ch-4 sp, ch 3, 2-dc Cl in same ch-4 sp (beg ch-3 and following 2-dc Cl count as first 3-dc Cl), ch 4, sc in next ch-4 sp, ch 4, (3-dc Cl, ch 4, 3-dc Cl) in next corner ch-4 sp, *ch 4, sc in next ch-4 sp, ch 4, 3-dc Cl in next ch-4 sp, ch 4, sc in next ch-4 sp, ch 4, (3-dc Cl, ch 4, 3-dc Cl) in next corner ch-4 sp; rep from * 2 more times, ch 4, sc in next ch-4 sp, ch 4; join with sl st in first cluster – 4 (3-dc Cl, ch 4, 3-dc Cl) corners, 16 ch-4 sps, four 3-dc Cl, and 8 sc.
Fasten off.

Second Flower Square

Ch 5; join with sl st in first ch to form a ring.

Rnds 1-3: Work same as Rnds 1-3 of First Flower Square.
Note: Rnd 4 is worked the same as Rnd 4 of First Flower Square EXCEPT that one side edge of Second Flower Square is joined to one side edge of First Flower Square using ch-4 joins (see Stitch Guide on page 10).

Rnd 4 (joining rnd):

Work to 2nd corner: Sl st in first 2 ch of first ch-4 sp, ch 3, 2-dc Cl in same ch-4 sp (beg ch-3 and following 2-dc Cl count as first 3-dc Cl), ch 4, sc in next ch-4 sp, ch 4, (3-dc Cl, ch 4, 3-dc Cl) in next corner ch-4 sp, ch 4, sc in next ch-4 sp, ch 4, 3-dc Cl in next ch-4 sp, ch 4, sc in next ch-4 sp, ch 4;

Work along next edge AND join the edge to ONE edge of previous Flower Square: 3-dc Cl in next corner ch-4 sp, ch-4 join, 3-dc Cl in same corner ch-4 sp, ch-4 join, sc in next ch-4 sp, ch-4 join, 3-dc Cl in next ch-4 sp, ch-4 join, sc in next ch-4 sp, ch-4 join, 3-dc Cl in next corner ch-4 sp, ch-4 join, 3-dc Cl in same corner ch-4 sp;

Work to end of rnd: Ch 4, sc in next ch-4 sp, ch 4, 3-dc Cl in next ch-4 sp, ch 4, sc in next ch-4 sp, ch 4, (3-dc Cl, ch 4, 3-dc Cl) in next corner ch-4 sp, ch 4, sc in next ch-4 sp, ch 4; join with sl st in first cluster.

Fasten off.

Third Flower Square

Make same as Second Flower Square, joining one side edge of current Flower Square to one side edge of previous Flower Square to form a strip.

Fourth Flower Square

Make same as Second Flower Square, joining one side edge of current Flower Square to one side edge of First Flower Square, to beg next row of Flower Squares.

Fifth Flower Square

Ch 5; join with sl st in first ch to form a ring.

Rnds 1-3: Work same as Rnds 1-3 of First Flower Square.

Note: Rnd 4 is worked the same as Rnd 4 of First Flower Square, EXCEPT that two side edges of current Flower Square are joined to one side edge of Second Flower Square and one side edge of Fourth Flower Square.

Rnd 4 (joining rnd):

Work to 2nd corner: Sl st in first 2 ch of first ch-4 sp, ch 3, 2-dc Cl in same ch-4 sp (beg ch-3 and following 2-dc Cl count as first 3-dc Cl), ch 4, sc in next ch-4 sp, ch 4, (3-dc Cl, ch 4, 3-dc Cl) in next corner ch-4 sp, ch 4, sc in next ch-4 sp, ch 4, 3-dc Cl in next ch-4 sp, ch 4, sc in next ch-4 sp, ch 4;

Work along next 2 edges AND join each of these edges to one edge of 2 previous Flower Squares: 3-dc Cl in next corner ch-4 sp, ch-4 join, 3-dc Cl in same corner ch-4 sp, *ch-4 join, sc in next ch-4 sp, ch-4 join, 3-dc Cl in next ch-4 sp, ch-4 join, sc in next ch-4 sp, ch-4 join, 3-dc Cl in next corner ch-4 sp, ch-4 join, 3-dc Cl in same corner ch-4 sp; rep from * once more;

Work to end of rnd: Ch 4, sc in next ch-4 sp, ch 4; join with sl st in first cluster.

Fasten off.

Sixth Flower Square

Make same as Fifth Flower Square, joining one side edge of current Flower Square to one side edge of Third Flower Square and next side edge to Fifth Flower Square.

Seventh, Eighth, and Ninth Flower Squares

Make same as Fourth, Fifth, and Sixth Flower Squares, joining to previous row of Flower Squares to complete a 3rd row of Flower Squares.

Tenth, Eleventh, and Twelfth Flower Squares

Make same as Fourth, Fifth, and Sixth Flower Squares, joining to previous row of Flower Squares to complete a 4th row of Flower Squares.

Thirteenth, Fourteenth, and Fifteenth Flower Squares

Make same as Fourth, Fifth, and Sixth Flower Squares, joining to previous row of Flower Squares to complete a 5th row of Flower Squares.

Neck

Row 1 (RS): From RS, join yarn with sc in top right corner ch-4 sp, *ch 2, sk next Cl, 2-dc Cl in next ch-4 sp, ch 2, sc in next sc, ch 2, 2-dc Cl in next ch-4 sp, ch 2, sc in next Cl, ch 2, 2-dc Cl in next ch-4 sp, ch 2, sc in next sc, ch 2, 2-dc Cl in next ch-4 sp, ch 2 **, sk next Cl, sc in join between Flower Squares; rep from * across top edge ending last rep at **, sc in top left corner ch-4 sp – 12 Cl, 24 ch-2 sps, and 13 sc.

Rows 2-6: Beg with Row 2 of pattern, work in Lace pattern for 5 rows – 11 ch-5 sps, 12 sc, 2 ch-2 sps, and 2 dc in Row 6.

Right Shoulder

Row 1 (RS): Ch 1, turn, sc in first dc, sk first ch-2 sp, (ch 2, 2-dc Cl in next sc, ch 2, sc in next ch-5 sp) 3 times; leave rem sts unworked for back neck and left shoulder – 3 Cl, 6 ch-2 sps, and 4 sc.

Row 2: Ch 1, turn, sk first sc, sl st in next 2 ch, sc in next Cl, (ch 5, sc in next Cl) twice, ch 2, sk last ch-2 sp, dc in last sc – 2 ch-5 sps, 3 sc, 1 ch-2 sp, and 1 dc.
Fasten off.

Left Shoulder

Row 1 (RS): Sk first 5 unworked ch-5 sps following right shoulder, join yarn with sc in next ch-5 sp, (ch 2, 2-dc Cl in next sc, ch 2, sc in next ch-5 sp) 3 times working last sc in 3rd ch of beg ch-5 – 3 Cl, 6 ch-2 sps and 4 sc.

Row 2: Ch 5 (counts as dc, ch 2), turn, sc in next Cl, (ch 5, sc in next Cl) twice; leave rem sts unworked – 2 ch-5 sps, 3 sc, 1 ch-2 sp, and 1 dc.
Fasten off.

FRONT

Make same as Back to Neck.

Neck

Row 1 (RS): From RS, join yarn with sc in top right corner ch-4 sp, *ch 2, sk next Cl, 2-dc Cl in next ch-4 sp, ch 2, sc in next sc, ch 2, 2-dc Cl in next ch-4 sp, ch 2, sc in next Cl, ch 2, 2-dc Cl in next ch-4 sp, ch 2, sc in next sc, ch 2, 2-dc Cl in next ch-4 sp, ch 2 **, sk next Cl, sc in join between Flower Squares; rep from * across top edge ending last rep at **, sc in top left corner ch-4 sp – 12 Cl, 24 ch-2 sps, and 13 sc.

Row 2: Work Row 2 of Lace pattern – 11 ch-5 sps, 12 sc, 2 ch-2 sps, and 2 dc.

Left Shoulder

Row 1 (RS): Ch 1, turn, sc in first dc, sk first ch-2 sp, (ch 2, 2-dc Cl in next sc, ch 2, sc in next ch-5 sp) 5 times; leave rem sts unworked for front neck and right shoulder – 5 Cl, 10 ch-2 sps, and 6 sc.

Row 2: Ch 1, turn, sk first sc, sl st in next 2 ch, sc in next Cl, (ch 5, sc in next Cl) 4 times, ch 2, sk last ch-2 sp, dc in last sc – 4 ch-5 sps, 5 sc, 1 ch-2 sp, and 1 dc.

Row 3: Ch 1, turn, sc in first dc, sk first ch-2 sp, (ch 2, 2-dc Cl in next sc, ch 2, sc in next ch-5 sp) 4 times; leave rem sts unworked – 4 Cl, 8 ch-2 sps, and 5 sc.

Row 4: Ch 1, turn, sk first sc, sl st in next 2 ch, sc in next Cl, (ch 5, sc in next Cl) 3 times, ch 2, sk last ch-2 sp, dc in last sc – 3 ch-5 sps, 4 sc, 1 ch-2 sp, and 1 dc.

Row 5: Ch 1, turn, sc in first dc, sk first ch-2 sp, (ch 2, 2-dc Cl in next sc, ch 2, sc in next ch-5 sp) 3 times; leave rem sts unworked – 3 Cl, 6 ch-2 sps, and 4 sc.

Row 6: Ch 1, turn, sk first sc, sl st in next 2 ch, sc in next Cl, (ch 5, sc in next Cl) twice, ch 2, sk last ch-2 sp, dc in last sc – 2 ch-5 sps, 3 sc, 1 ch-2 sp, and 1 dc.

Shoulder Joining Row: Hold Front and Back with RS tog and sts matching. Working from WS and through both thicknesses, ch 1, turn, sc in first st, (ch 5, sc in next ch-5 sp) twice.
Fasten off.

Right Shoulder

Row 1 (RS): Sk first unworked ch-5 sp following left shoulder, join yarn with sc in next ch-5 sp, (ch 2, 2-dc Cl in next sc, ch 2, sc in next ch-5 sp) 5 times working last sc in 3rd ch of beg ch-5 – 5 Cl, 10 ch-2 sps, and 6 sc.

Row 2: Ch 5 (counts as dc, ch 2), turn, sk first ch-2 sp, sc in next Cl, (ch 5, sc in next Cl) 4 times; leave rem sts unworked – 4 ch-5 sps, 5 sc, 1 ch-2 sp, and 1 dc.

Row 3: Ch 1, turn, sk first sc, sl st in next 2 ch, sc in next ch, (ch 2, 2-dc Cl in next sc, ch 2, sc in next ch-5 sp) 4 times working last sc in 3rd ch of beg ch-5 – 4 Cl, 8 ch-2 sps, and 5 sc.

Row 4: Ch 5 (counts as dc, ch 2), turn, sk first ch-2 sp, sc in next Cl, (ch 5, sc in next Cl) 3 times; leave rem sts unworked – 3 ch-5 sps, 4 sc, 1 ch-2 sp, and 1 dc.

Row 5: Ch 1, turn, sk first sc, sl st in next 2 ch, sc in next ch, (ch 2, 2-dc Cl in next sc, ch 2, sc in next ch-5 sp) 3 times working last sc in 3rd ch of beg ch-5 – 3 Cl, 6 ch-2 sps, and 4 sc.

Row 6: Ch 5 (counts as dc, ch 2), turn, sk first ch-2 sp, sc in next Cl, (ch 5, sc in next Cl) twice; leave rem sts unworked – 2 ch-5 sps, 3 sc, 1 ch-2 sp, and 1 dc.

Shoulder Joining Row: Hold Front and Back with RS tog and sts matching. Sl st in first 2 ch of first ch-5 sp of Front; working from WS and through both thicknesses, sc in first ch-5 sp, ch 5, sc in next ch-5 sp, ch 5, sc in last st.
Fasten off.

Sides

Row 1 (RS): From RS, join yarn with sc in one lower corner ch-4 sp of Front so that you are ready to work up the side edge, *ch 2, sk next Cl, 2-dc Cl in next ch-4 sp, ch 2, sc in next sc, ch 2, 2-dc Cl in next ch-4 sp, ch 2, sc in next Cl, ch 2, 2-dc Cl in next ch-4 sp, ch 2, sc in next sc, ch 2, 2-dc Cl in next ch-4 sp, ch 2 **, sk next Cl, sc in join between Flower Squares; rep from * along side edge of Front ending last rep at **; working in ends of rows of Front neck and shoulder, sc in end of first row, sk next row, (ch 2, 2-dc Cl in end of next row, ch 2, sc in end of next row) twice, ch 2, 2-dc Cl in end of next row, ch 2, sk end of next row, sc in end of Shoulder Joining Row; working in ends of rows of Back shoulder, sk next row, (ch 2, 2-dc Cl in end of next row, ch 2, sc in end of next row) twice, ch 2, 2-dc Cl in end of next row, ch 2, sk end of next row, sc in end of last row; work along side edge of Back in same way as you worked along side edge of Front ending with sc in lower corner ch-4 sp of Back – 46 Cl, 92 ch-2 sps, and 47 sc.

Rows 2-6{12-18}: Beg with Row 2 of pattern, work in Lace pattern for 5{11-17} rows – you will have 46 sc, 45 ch-5 sps, 2 ch-2 sps, and 2 dc in WS rows.
Fasten off.

Rep along 2nd side edge beg in lower Back corner ch-4 sp.

SLEEVES

Row 1 (RS): From RS of Front and working along side edge of Front, join yarn with sc in 16th{15th-14th} ch-5 sp above lower edge, (ch 2, 2-dc Cl in next sc, ch 2, sc in next ch-5 sp) 14{16-18} times; leave rem 15{14-13} ch-5 sps unworked – 14{16-18} Cl, 28{32-36} ch-2 sps, and 15{17-19} sc.

Rows 2-4: Beg with Row 2 of pattern, work in Lace pattern for 3 rows – 14{16-18} sc, 13{15-17} ch-5 sps, 2 ch-2 sps, and 2 dc.

Row 5: Ch 1, turn, sl st in first ch-2 sp, *ch 2, 2-dc Cl in next sc, ch 2, sc in next ch-5 sp; rep from * to last sc, ch 2, 2-dc Cl in last sc, ch 2, sl st in last ch-sp; leave rem st unworked – 14{16-18} Cl, 26{30-34} ch-2 sps, and 13{15-17} sc.

Row 6: Ch 1, turn, sk sl st, sl st in next 2 ch, sc in first Cl, *ch 5, sc in next Cl; rep from * across, leave beg ch-2 unworked – 14{16-18} sc and 13{15-17} ch-5 sps.

Row 7: Ch 2, dc in first st (beg ch-2 and following dc count as first Cl), turn, *ch 2, sc in next ch-5 sp, ch 2, 2-dc Cl in next sc; rep from * across – 14{16-18} Cl, 26{30-34} ch-2 sps, and 13{15-17} sc.

Row 8: Ch 1, turn, sc in first Cl, *ch 5, sc in next Cl; rep from * across.

Row 9: Ch 1, turn, sl st in first 2 ch of first ch-5 sp, sc in same ch-5 sp, *ch 2, 2-dc Cl in next sc, ch 2, sc in next ch-5 sp; rep from * across; leave last st unworked – 12{14-16} Cl, 24{28-32} ch-2 sps, and 13{15-17} sc.

Rows 10-14: Beg with Row 2 of pattern, work in Lace pattern for 5 rows – 12{14-16} sc, 11{13-15} ch-5 sps, 2 ch-2 sps, and 2 dc in WS rows.

Rows 15-19: Rep Rows 5-9 – 10{12-14} Cl, 20{24-28} ch-2 sps, and 11{13-15} sc in Row 19.

Rows 20-28: Beg with Row 2 of pattern, work in Lace pattern for 9 rows – 10{12-14} sc, 9{11-13} ch-5 sps, 2 ch-2 sps and 2 dc in WS rows.

Rows 29-33: Rep Rows 5-9 – 8{10-12} Cl, 16{20-24} ch-2 sps, and 9{11-13} sc in Row 33.

Rows 34-42: Beg with Row 2 of pattern, work in Lace pattern for 9 rows – 8{10-12} sc, 7{9-11} ch-5 sps, 2 ch-2 sps and 2 dc in WS rows.

Last Row: Ch 1, turn, sc in first dc, ch 2, sc in next sc, *ch 5, sc in next sc; rep from * to beg ch-5, ch 2, sc in 3rd ch of beg ch-5.
Do NOT fasten off.

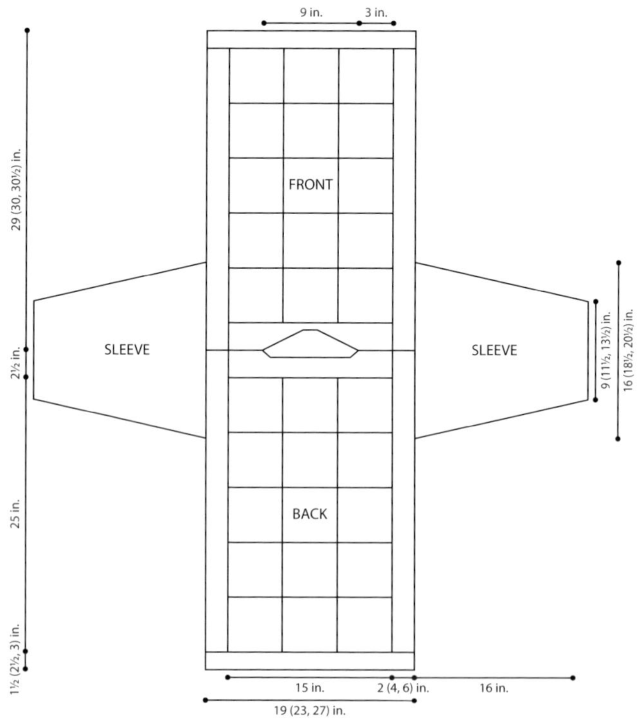

Sleeve and Side Seams

Fold piece in half along shoulder line and match ends of rows and sts along Sleeve and side edges. Working through both thicknesses, sc in end of last row of Sleeve, work (ch 3, sc in edge) evenly spaced along Sleeve edge and side edge to about 5½{4½-4}"/14{11.5-10} cm) above lower edge, leave rem of side edge unjoined for side slit.
Fasten off.

Rep Sleeve on other side, beg in 16th{15th-14th} ch-5 sp of side edge of Back above lower edge.

Lower Edging

Row 1 (RS): From RS, join yarn with a sc in beg corner of lower edge of Front; working in ends of rows of sides, (ch 2, 2-dc Cl in end of next row, ch 2, sc in end of next row) 3{6-9} times working last sc in corner ch-3 sp of Flower Square, *ch 2, sk next Cl, 2-dc Cl in next ch-4 sp, ch 2, sc in next sc, ch 2, 2-dc Cl in next ch-4 sp, ch 2, sc in next Cl, ch 2, 2-dc Cl in next ch-4 sp, ch 2, sc in next sc, ch 2, 2-dc Cl in next ch-4 sp, ch 2 **, sk next Cl, sc in join between Flower Squares; rep from * across lower edge ending last rep at **, sc in corner ch-4 sp; working in ends of rows of Side, (ch 2, 2-dc Cl in end of next row, ch 2, sc in end of next row) 3{6-9} times.

Rows 2-4{6-8}: Beg with Row 2 of pattern, work in Lace pattern for 3{5-7} rows.
Fasten off.

Rep Lower Edging along lower edge of Back.
Do NOT fasten off.

Last Rnd (RS): Ch 1, turn, *sc in first dc, ch 2, sc in next sc, **ch 5, sc in next sc; rep from ** to beg ch-5, ch 2, sc in 3rd ch of beg ch-5; working up one side of slit and down the other, ch 2, sc in end of next row, (ch 5, sc in edge) as evenly spaced as possible to end of slit, ch 2; rep from * along lower edge of Front and 2nd side slit; join with sl st in first sc.
Fasten off.

FINISHING

Neck Edging

Row 1 (RS): From RS, join with sc in neck edge at one shoulder seam, *ch 5, sc in edge; rep from * as evenly spaced as possible around neck edge; join with sl st in first sc.
Fasten off.

Weave in ends.

kimono Coverup

EASY +

SIZES

XS/S{M/L-1X/3X}

Finished Bust:

44{52-60}"/112{132-152.5} cm)

Finished Length:

28{28-28}"/71{71-71} cm

Note: Pattern is written for smallest size with changes for larger sizes in parentheses. When only one number is given, it applies to all sizes. To follow pattern more easily, circle all numbers pertaining to your size before beginning.

SHOPPING LIST

Yarn (Medium Weight) MEDIUM 4

LION BRAND® 24/7 COTTON®
(Art. #761)

- ☐ #149 Silver - 5{6-7} balls (A)
- ☐ #153 Black - 1{1-1} ball (B)
- ☐ #098 Ecru - 1{1-1} ball (C)

Crochet Hook

LION BRAND® crochet hook

- ☐ Size F-5 (3.75 mm)
  or size needed for gauge

Additional Supply

- ☐ LION BRAND® large-eyed blunt needle

GAUGE

1 Square = about 4½" x 4½" (11.5 cm x 11.5 cm).
4 V-sts = about 3" (7.5 cm);
8½ rows = about 4" (10 cm) in V-st pattern of sides and sleeves.

BE SURE TO CHECK YOUR GAUGE.

STITCH GUIDE

V-STITCH (abbreviated V-st)

(Dc, ch 1, dc) in indicated st or sp.

NOTES

1. Cover Up is made from 2 identical Halves.
2. Each Half begins with a Strip of 12 Granny Squares. Stitches are worked along one long edge of Strip for side and sleeve.

GRANNY SQUARE I (make 4)

With A, ch 4; join with sl st in first ch to form a ring.

Rnd 1 (RS): Ch 3 (counts as dc), 2 dc in ring, (ch 3, 3 dc in ring) 3 times, ch 3; join with sl st in top of beg ch-3 – you will have 12 dc and 4 ch-3 sps in this rnd (3 dc between ch-3 sps). Fasten off.

Rnd 2: From RS, draw up a loop of B in any ch-3 sp, ch 3 (counts as dc), (dc, ch 3, 2 dc) in same ch-3 sp, *dc in each dc to next ch-3 sp, (2 dc, ch 3, 2 dc) in ch-3 sp (corner made); rep from * 2 more times, dc in each dc to end of rnd; join with sl st in top of beg ch-3 – 28 dc and 4 corner ch-3 sps (7 dc between corner ch-3 sps). Fasten off.

Rnd 3: From RS, draw up a loop of C in any corner ch-3 sp, ch 6 (counts as dc, ch 3), dc in same corner ch-3 sp, *ch 1, dc in next dc, (ch 1, sk next dc, dc in next dc) 3 times, ch 1, (dc, ch 3, dc) in next corner ch-3 sp; rep from * 2 more times, ch 1, dc in next dc, (ch 1, sk next dc, dc in next dc) 3 times, ch 1; join with sl st in 3rd ch of beg ch-6 – 24 dc, 20 ch-1 sps, and 4 corner ch-3 sps (6 dc and 5 ch-1 sps between corner ch-3 sps). Do NOT fasten off.

Rnd 4: Sl st in first ch-sp, ch 3 (counts as dc), (dc, ch 3, 2 dc) in same corner ch-3 sp, *dc in each dc and ch-1 sp to next corner ch-3 sp, (2 dc, ch 3, 2 dc) in corner ch-3 sp; rep from * 2 more times, dc in each dc and ch-1 sp to end of rnd; join with sl st in top of beg ch-3 – 60 dc and 4 corner ch-3 sps (15 dc between corner ch-3 sps).
Fasten off.

GRANNY SQUARE II (make 4)

With A, ch 4; join with sl st in first ch to form a ring.

Rnd 1 (RS): Ch 3 (counts as dc), 2 dc in ring, (ch 3, 3 dc in ring) 3 times, ch 3; join with sl st in top of beg ch-3 – you will have 12 dc and 4 ch-3 sps in this rnd (3 dc between ch-3 sps).
Fasten off.

Rnd 2: From RS, draw up a loop of B in any ch-3 sp, ch 3 (counts as dc), (dc, ch 3, 2 dc) in same ch-3 sp, *dc in each dc to next ch-3 sp, (2 dc, ch 3, 2 dc) in ch-3 sp (corner made); rep from * 2 more times, dc in each dc to end of rnd; join with sl st in top of beg ch-3 – 28 dc and 4 corner ch-3 sps (7 dc between corner ch-3 sps).
Do NOT fasten off.

Rnd 3: Sl st in next dc, ch 4 (counts as dc, ch 1), (dc, ch 3, dc) in next corner ch-3 sp, *ch 1, dc in next dc, (ch 1, sk next dc, dc in next dc) 3 times, ch 1, (dc, ch 3, dc) in next corner ch-3 sp; rep from * 2 more times, ch 1, dc in next dc, (ch 1, sk next dc, dc in next dc) twice, ch 1, sk next dc; join with sl st in 3rd ch of beg ch-4 – 24 dc, 20 ch-1 sps, and 4 corner ch-3 sps (6 dc and 5 ch-1 sps between corner ch-3 sps).
Fasten off.

Rnd 4: From RS, draw up a loop of C in any corner ch-3 sp, ch 3 (counts as dc), (dc, ch 3, 2 dc) in same corner ch-3 sp, *dc in each dc and ch-1 sp to next corner ch-3 sp, (2 dc, ch 3, 2 dc) in corner ch-3 sp; rep from * 2 more times, dc in each dc and ch-1 sp to end of rnd; join with sl st in top of beg ch-3 – 60 dc and 4 corner ch-3 sps (15 dc between corner ch-3 sps).
Fasten off.

GRANNY SQUARE III (make 4)

Make same as Granny Square I using B for Rnd 1, C for Rnd 2, and A for Rnds 3 and 4.

GRANNY SQUARE IV (make 4)

Make same as Granny Square II using B for Rnd 1, C for Rnds 2 and 3, and A for Rnd 4.

GRANNY SQUARE V (make 4)

Make same as Granny Square I using C for Rnd 1, A for Rnd 2, and B for Rnds 3 and 4.

GRANNY SQUARE VI (make 4)

Make same as Granny Square II using C for Rnd 1, A for Rnds 2 and 3, and B for Rnd 4.

GRANNY SQUARE STRIPS (make 2)

Sew 12 Granny Squares into a strip in the following order: II, III, VI, I, IV, V, II, III, VI, I, IV, V.

HALF (make 2)

From RS, join A with sl st in corner ch-3 sp of last Square of one Strip, so that you are ready to work along one long edge.

Side

Row 1 (RS): Ch 3 (counts as dc), V-st in same corner ch-3 sp, (sk next 3 dc, V-st in next sp between sts) 4 times, sk next 3 dc, V-st in next corner ch-3 sp of same Square, *sk join between Squares, V-st in next corner ch-3 sp, (sk next 3 dc, V-st in next sp between sts) 4 times, sk next 3 dc, V-st in next corner ch-3 sp of same Square; rep from * across long edge of Strip, dc in same corner ch-3 sp as last V-st made – 72 V-sts and 1 dc at beg and end of row.

Row 2: Ch 3 (counts as dc), turn, *dc in first dc of next V-st, ch 1, sk ch-1 sp of same V-st, dc in 2nd dc of same V-st; rep from * to beg ch-3, dc in top of beg ch-3 – 146 dc and 72 ch-1 sps.

Row 3: Ch 3 (counts as dc), turn, V-st in each ch-1 sp to beg ch-3, dc in top of beg ch-3 – 72 V-sts and 1 dc at beg and end of row.

Rows 4-11{15-19}: Rep Rows 2 and 3 for 4{6-8} more times.

Row 12{16-20}: Rep Row 2. Fasten off.

Sleeve

From RS, draw up a loop of A in 49th{47th-45th} dc (this is the first dc of the 25th{24th-23rd} 2-dc group).

Row 1 (RS): Ch 3 (counts as dc), V-st in next 24{26-28} ch-1 sps, sk next dc, dc in next dc – 24{26-28} V sts and 1 dc at beg and end of row.

Row 2: Ch 3 (counts as dc), turn, *dc in first dc of next V-st, ch 1, sk ch-1 sp of same V-st, dc in 2nd dc of same V-st; rep from * to beg ch-3, dc in top of beg ch-3 – 50{54-58} dc and 24{26-28} ch-1 sps.

Row 3: Ch 3 (counts as dc), turn, V-st in each ch-1 sp to beg ch-3, dc in top of beg ch-3 – 24{26-28} V-sts and 1 dc at beg and end of row.

Rows 4-9: Rep Rows 2 and 3 for 3 more times.

Row 10: Rep Row 2. Fasten off.

Edging

From RS, draw up a loop in edge of last row of side so that you are ready to work in ends of rows towards unworked long edge of Granny Square Strip.

Note: When you see '0' repeats in an instruction, this means that you should not perform that particular instruction, just skip to the next part of the instruction.

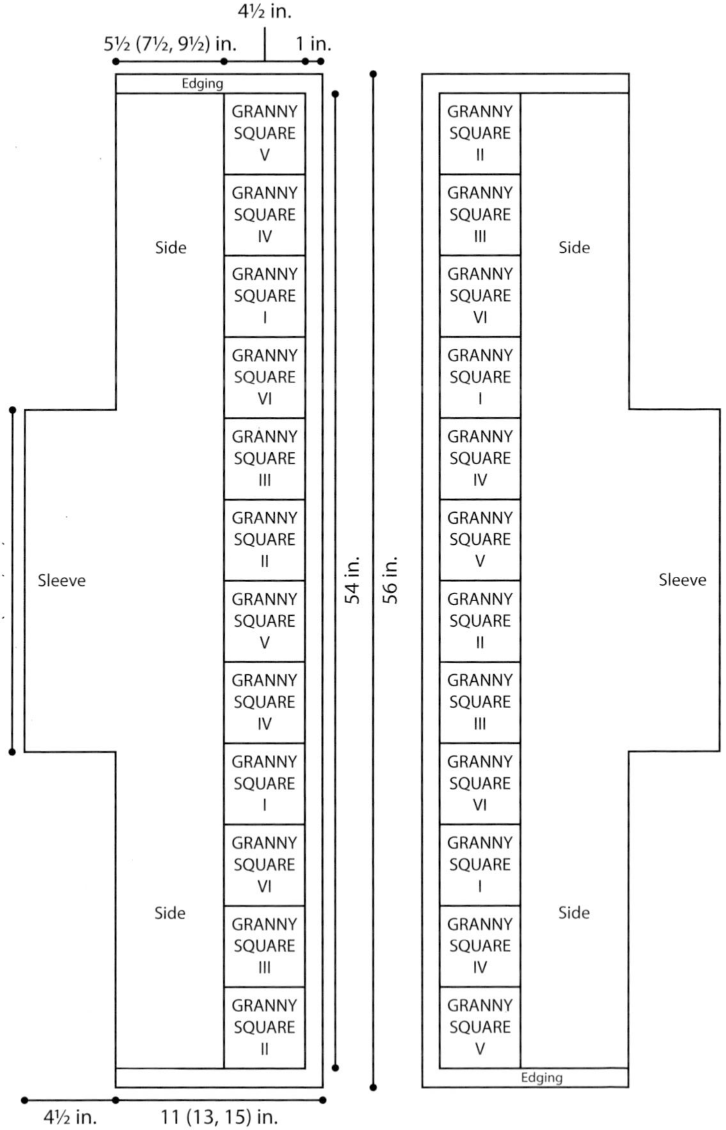

Row 1: Ch 3 (counts as dc), working in ends of rows of side, V-st in end of first row, (sk next row, V-st in end of each of next 2 rows) 3{4-6} times, sk next 1{2-0} rows, V-st in end of last row; working across short end of Granny Strip, V-st in corner ch-3 sp, (sk next 3 dc, V-st in next sp between sts) 4 times, sk next 3 dc, 3 V-st in corner ch-3 sp; working along long edge of Strip, (sk next 3 dc, V-st in next sp between sts) 4 times, sk next 3 dc, V-st in corner ch-3 sp of same Square, *sk join between Squares, V-st in corner ch-3 sp of next Square, (sk next 3 dc, V-st in next sp between sts) 4 times, sk next 3 dc, V-st in corner ch-3 sp of same Square; rep from * across long edge of Strip, work 2 more V-sts in same corner ch-3 sp as last V-st made; working across short end of Granny Strip (sk next 3 dc, V-st in next sp between sts) 4 times, sk next 3 dc, V-st in corner ch-3 sp; working in ends of rows along side, work same as for first side.

Row 2: Ch 3 (counts as dc), turn, *dc in first dc of next V-st, ch 1, sk ch-1 sp of same V-st, dc in 2nd dc of same V-st; rep from * all the way across working (2 dc, ch 1, 2 dc) in ch-1 sp of center V-st of each 3 V-st corner. Fasten off.

FINISHING

Fold one Half along shoulder line and sew side and sleeve seams, leaving about 8" (20.5 cm) unsewn at lower edge for side slit.
Repeat to fold and seam second Half.

Join Halves and Edge Piece

Arrange Halves so that Granny Strip edgings are side by side.

From WS and working through both thicknesses, join A with sl st in inner corner at one end of Granny Strip edging, working along long edge, ch 1, sc in corner ch-1 sp, *ch 2, sc in next ch-1 sp; rep from * 32 more times for back seam; working in edge of one Half only, **ch 2, sc in next ch-1 sp; rep from ** evenly spaced all the way along front edge, lower edges and slit edges back to back seam; join with sl st in first sc.
Fasten off.

Weave in ends.

openwork Top

EASY +

SIZES

XS/S{M/L-1X/3X}

Finished Bust:

36{45-52}"/91.5{114.5-132} cm)

Finished Length:

21½{22½-23½}"/54.5{57-59.5} cm

Note: Pattern is written for smallest size with changes for larger sizes in parentheses. When only one number is given, it applies to all sizes. To follow pattern more easily, circle all numbers pertaining to your size before beginning.

SHOPPING LIST

Yarn (Medium Weight) MEDIUM 4

LION BRAND® 24/7 COTTON®

(Art. #761)

- ☐ #108 Denim 4{5, 6} balls

Crochet Hook

LION BRAND® crochet hook

- ☐ Size G-6 (4.25 mm)
  or size needed for gauge

Additional Supply

- ☐ LION BRAND® large-eyed blunt needle

GAUGE

13½ sts + 8 rows = about 4" (10 cm) in V-st Pattern.

13½ sts + 10 rows = about 4" (10 cm) in Sc/Chain Pattern.

BE SURE TO CHECK YOUR GAUGE.

STITCH GUIDE

V-STITCH (abbreviated V-st)

Work 2 dc in same indicated space.

PATTERN STITCH

V-st Pattern

Row 1: Ch 3 (counts as dc), turn, V-st in sp between sts of each V-st across, dc in top of beg ch-3.

Rep Row 1 for V-st Pattern.

Sc/Chain Pattern

Row 1: Ch 1, turn, sc in first st, *ch 3, sk next ch-3 sp, (sc, ch 3, sc) in next ch-3 sp; rep from * to last ch-3 sp, ch 3, sk last ch-3 sp, sc in last st.

Rep Row 1 for Sc/Chain Pattern.

NOTES

1. Top is made in 2 pieces: Back and Front.
2. Both pieces are worked from lower edge upwards. At underarms, chains are worked on each side edge for sleeves.
3. Lower edging is worked onto completed Back and Front.

BACK

Ch 63{79-91}.

Row 1 (RS): Work V-st in 5th ch from hook (4 skipped ch count as 1 base ch and first dc), *sk next ch, V-st in next ch; rep from * to last 2 ch, sk next ch, dc in last ch – you will have 29{37-43} V-sts and a dc at the beg and end of this row.

Rows 2-18: Work in V-st Pattern for 17 rows.

Shape Sleeves

Drop loop from hook and enlarge it so that it does not unravel. With a separate length of yarn, ch 7 for underarm ch, join ch-7 with sl st to first st of Row 18.

Fasten off.

Return dropped loop to hook.

Row 19: Ch 9 for underarm ch, turn, V-st in 5th ch from hook (4 skipped ch count as 1 base ch and first dc), (sk next ch, V-st in next ch) twice, sk first dc, V-st in sp between sts of each V-st across to beg ch-3, sk beg ch-3, V-st in next ch, (sk next ch, V-st in next ch) twice, sk next ch, dc in last ch – 35{43-49} V-sts.

Rows 20-22{24-26}: Work in V-st Pattern for 3{5-7} rows.

Next Row: Ch 1, turn, sc in first st, *ch 3, sk next V-st, (sc, ch 3, sc) in sp between sts of next V-st; rep from * to last V-st, ch 3, sk last V-st, sc in last st – 17{21-24} (sc, ch 3, sc) groups.

Work in Sc/Chain Pattern for 13 rows.

Last Row: Ch 1, turn, sc in first st, *ch 3, sk next ch-3 sp, sc in next ch-3 sp; rep from * to last ch-3 sp, ch 3, sk last ch-3 sp, sc in last st. Fasten off.

Lower Edging

Row 1 (RS): From RS and working along opposite side of foundation ch, join yarn with sc in ch at base of first st, *ch 3, sk next 3 ch, (sc, ch 3, sc) in ch at base of next V-st; rep from * to ch before ch at base of last V-st, ch 3, sk next 3 ch, sc in next ch – 14{18-21} (sc, ch 3, sc) groups.

Rows 2-10: Work in Sc/Chain Pattern for 9 rows.

Row 11: Ch 1, turn, sc in first st, *ch 3, sk next ch-3 sp, sc in next ch-3 sp; rep from * to last ch-3 sp, ch 3, sk last ch-3 sp, sc in last st.
Fasten off.

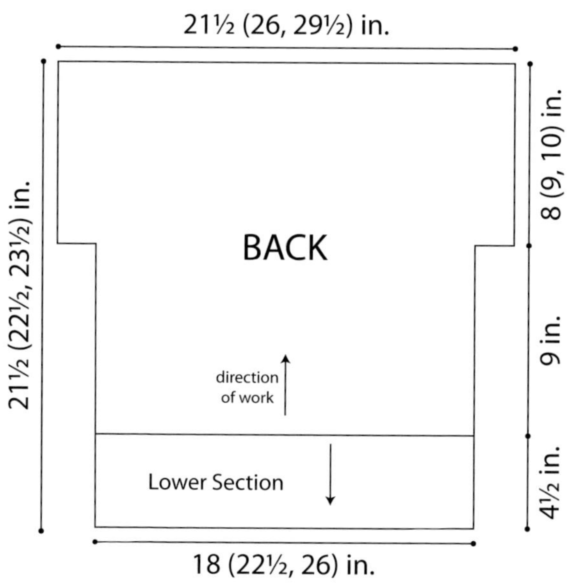

FRONT

Make same as Back through Row 22{24-26}.

Next Row (RS): Ch 1, turn, sc in first st, *ch 3, sk next V-st, (sc, ch 3, sc) in sp between sts of next V-st; rep from * to last 4 sts, ch 3, sk next V-st, sc in last st – 17{21-24} (sc, ch 3, sc) groups.

Work in Sc/Chain Pattern for 11 rows.

Left Shoulder

Row 1 (RS): Ch 1, turn, sc in first st, *ch 3, sk next ch-3 sp, (sc, ch 3, sc) in next ch-3 sp; rep from * 3{5-6} more times, ch 3, sk next ch-3 sp, sc in next ch-3 sp; leave rem sts unworked for front neck and right shoulder – 4{6-7} (sc, ch 3, sc) groups.

Row 2: Work in Sc/Chain Pattern for 1 row.

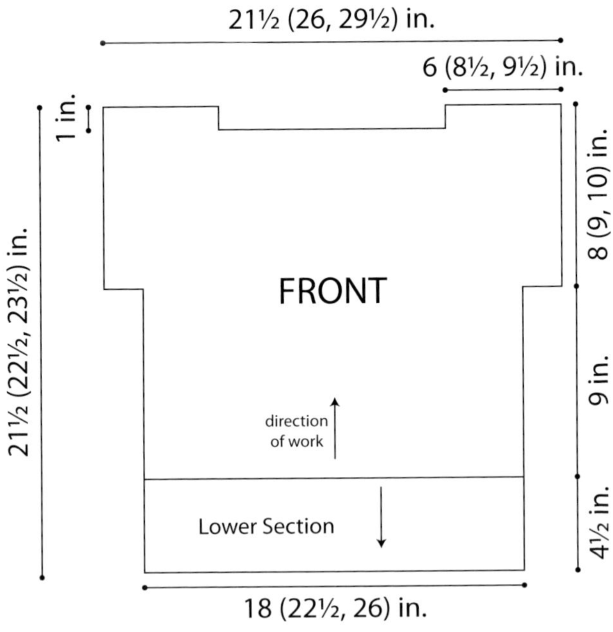

Row 3: Ch 1, turn, sc in first st, *ch 3, sk next ch-3 sp, sc in next ch-3 sp; rep from * to last ch-3 sp, ch 3, sk last ch-3 sp, sc in last st.
Fasten off.

Right Shoulder

Row 1 (RS): From RS, sk first 15{15-17} unworked ch-3 sps following Row 1 of left shoulder, join yarn with a sc in next ch-3 sp, *ch 3, sk next ch-3 sp, (sc, ch 3, sc) in next ch-3 sp; rep from * to last ch-3 sp, ch 3, sk last ch-3 sp, sc in last st – 4{6-7} (sc, ch 3, sc) groups.

Row 2: Work in Sc/Chain Pattern for 1 row.

Row 3: Ch 1, turn, sc in first st, *ch 3, sk next ch-3 sp, sc in next ch-3 sp; rep from * to last ch-3 sp, ch 3, sk last ch-3 sp, sc in last st.
Fasten off.

Front Neck

From RS, join yarn with a sl st in last st of Row 1 of left shoulder, *ch 3, sk next ch-3 sp, sc in next ch-3 sp; rep from * to last ch-3 sp before beg of right shoulder, ch 3, sk next ch-3 sp, sl st in first st of right shoulder.
Fasten off.

Lower Edging

Work same as Back lower edging.

FINISHING

Join Shoulders

Hold Front and Back with RS together. With WS of Back facing you and working through both thicknesses, join yarn with a sc in first st, (ch 3, sk next ch-3 sp, sc in next sc) to end of first shoulder; working across Back neck edge only, (ch 3, sk next ch-3 sp, sc in next sc) to last ch-3 sp of Back neck edge; working through both thicknesses, (ch 3, sk next ch-3 sp, sc in next sc) to end of 2nd shoulder.
Fasten off.

Front Neck Edging

From RS, join yarn with a sl st in neck edge at left shoulder seam. Working in ends of rows along left front neck edge, ch 3, sk end of next row, sc in end of next row; working along front neck edge, *ch 3, sk next ch-3 sp, sc in next sc; rep from * to last ch-3 sp of Front neck edge, ch 3, sk next ch-3 sp; working in ends of rows along right front neck edge, sc in end of next row, ch 3, sk end of next row, sl st in right shoulder seam.
Fasten off.

Sew side and sleeve seams.

Weave in ends.

fringed Tank Top

EASY +

SIZES

XS/S{M/L-1X/3X}

Finished Bust:

36{45-52}"/91.5{114.5-132} cm)

Finished Length:

23{23½-24½}"/58.5{59.5-62} cm), not including fringe

Note: Pattern is written for smallest size with changes for larger sizes in parentheses. When only one number is given, it applies to all sizes. To follow pattern more easily, circle all numbers pertaining to your size before beginning.

SHOPPING LIST

Yarn (Medium Weight) 4 MEDIUM

LION BRAND® 24/7 COTTON® (Art. #761)

- ☐ #144 Magenta - 4{5-6} balls

Crochet Hook

LION BRAND® crochet hook

- ☐ Size G-6 (4.25 mm) **or** size needed for gauge

Additional Supplies

- ☐ LION BRAND® large-eyed blunt needle
- ☐ LION BRAND® split ring markers

GAUGE

14½ sts + 10½ rows = about 4" (10 cm) in Sc/Dc Pattern.

BE SURE TO CHECK YOUR GAUGE.

STITCH GUIDE

DOUBLE CROCHET 2 STITCHES TOGETHER (abbreviated dc2tog)

(Yarn over, insert hook in next st and draw up a loop, yarn over and draw through 2 loops) twice, yarn over and draw through all 3 loops on hook – 1 st decreased.

SINGLE CROCHET 2 STITCHES TOGETHER (abbreviated sc2tog)

(Insert hook in next st and draw up a loop) twice, yarn over and draw through all 3 loops on hook – 1 st decreased.

PATTERN STITCH

Sc/Dc Pattern (worked over an odd number of sts)

Row 1 (RS): Ch 1, turn, sc in each st and ch-1 sp to end of row.

Row 2: Ch 3 (counts as dc), turn, dc in each st to marked center st, ch 1, sk center st, dc in each st to end of row.

Rep Rows 1 and 2 for Sc/Dc pattern.

NOTES

1. Tank Top is made in 2 pieces: Back and Front.
2. Back and Front are both worked from the lower edge upwards.
3. An edging is worked around neck and armhole edges, then fringe is added to the lower edge.

BACK

Ch 68{84-98}.

Row 1 (RS): Sc in 2nd ch from hook and in each ch across – you will have 67{83-97} sc in this row.

Row 2: Ch 4 (counts as dc, ch 1), turn, sk first 2 sts, dc in next st, *ch 1, sk next st, dc in next st; rep from * to end of row – 34{42-49} dc and 33{41-48} ch-1 sps.

Row 3: Ch 1, turn, sc in first st, *sc in next ch-1 sp, sc in next st; rep from * to end of row – 67{83-97} sc.

Row 4: Ch 3 (counts as dc), turn, dc in next 32{40-47} sts, ch 1, sk next st, dc in each st to end of row – 66{82-96} dc and 1 ch-1 sp. Place a marker in the center ch-1 sp. Move the marker up as each row is worked.

Rows 5 and 6: Work Rows 1 and 2 of Sc/Dc pattern.

Shape Waist

Row 7 (Decrease Row – RS): Ch 1, turn, sc in first 3 sts, sc2tog, sc in each st and ch-1 sp to last 5 sts, sc2tog, sc in last 3 sts – 65{81-95} sc.

Rows 8-12: Beg with Row 2 of pattern, work in Sc/Dc pattern for 5 rows – 64{80-94} dc and 1 ch-1 sp in Row 12.

Rows 13-24: Rep Rows 7-12 twice – 60{76-90} dc and 1 ch-1 sp in Row 24.

Rows 25-28: Beg with Row 1 of pattern, work in Sc/Dc pattern for 4 rows.

Row 29 (Increase Row): Ch 1, turn, sc in first 3 sts, 2 sc in next st, sc in each st and ch-1 sp to last 4 sts, 2 sc in next st, sc in last 3 sts – 63{79-93} sc.

Rows 30-34: Beg with Row 2 of pattern, work in Sc/Dc pattern for 5 rows.

Rows 35-40: Rep Rows 29-34 – 64{80-94} sc and 1 ch-1 sp in Row 40.

Shape Armholes

Row 41 (RS): Ch 1, turn, sl st in first 8{10-12} sts, sc in each st and ch-1 sp to last 8{10-12} sts; leave last 8{10-12} sts unworked – 49{61-71} sts.

Row 42 (Decrease Row): Ch 3 (counts as dc), turn, dc2tog, dc in each st to marked center st, ch 1, sk center st, dc in each st to last 3 sts, dc2tog, dc in last st – 46{58-68} sts and 1 ch-1 sp.

Row 43 (Decrease Row): Ch 1, turn, sk first st, sc2tog, sc in each st and ch-1 sp to last 4 sts, sc2tog, sk next st, sc in last st – 43{55-65} sts.

Row 44 (Decrease Row): Rep Row 42 – 40{52-62} sts and 1 ch-1 sp.

Row 45 (Decrease Row): Ch 1, turn, sk first st, sc in each st to last 2 sts, sk next st, sc in last st – 39{51-61} sts.

Size XS/S Only

Beg with Row 2 of pattern, work in Sc/Dc pattern for 9 rows.

Sizes M/L{1X/3X} Only

Rows 46-47{49}: Rep Rows 44 and 45 for 1{2} more time(s) – 47{53} sts. Beg with Row 2 of pattern, work in Sc/Dc pattern for 9 rows.

Shape Neck

Right Shoulder

Row 1 (RS): Ch 1, turn, sc in first 7{9-11} sts, sc2tog, sc in next st; leave rem sts unworked for back neck and left shoulder – 9{11-13} sts.

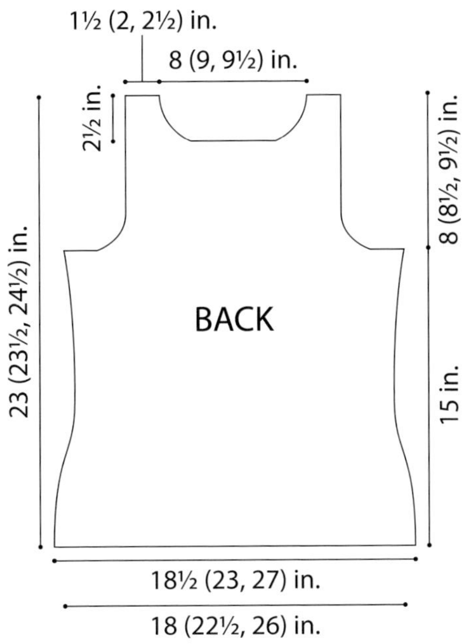

Row 2: Ch 3 (counts as dc), turn, dc2tog, dc in each st to end of row – 8{10-12} sts.

Row 3: Ch 1, turn, sc in each st to last 2 sts, sk next st, sc in last st – 7{9-11} sts.

Rows 4 and 5: Rep Rows 2 and 3 – 5{7, 9} sts in Row 5.

Row 6: Ch 3 (counts as dc), turn, dc in each st to end of row.
Fasten off.

Left Shoulder

Row 1 (RS): From RS, sk first 19{23-25} unworked sts following Row 1 of right shoulder, join yarn with a sc in next st, sc2tog, sc in each st to end of row – 9{11-13} sts.

Row 2: Ch 3 (counts as dc), turn, dc in each st to last 3 sts, dc2tog, dc in last st – 8{10-12} sts.

Row 3: Ch 1, turn, sk first st, sc in each st to end of row – 7{9-11} sts.

Rows 4 and 5: Rep Rows 2 and 3 – 5{7-9} sts in Row 5.

Row 6: Ch 3 (counts as dc), turn, dc in each st to end of row.
Fasten off.

FRONT

Work same as Back until you have completed Row 42 – 46{58-68} sts and 1 ch-1 sp.

Shape Neck and Continue Shaping Armhole

Shape Left Shoulder

Row 43 (RS): Ch 1, turn, sk first st, sc2tog, sc in next 16{22-27} sts, sc2tog, sc in next st; leave rem sts unworked for front neck and right shoulder – 19{25-30} sts.

Row 44 (Decrease Row): Ch 3 (counts as dc), turn, dc2tog, dc in each st to last 3 sts, dc2tog, dc in last st – 17{23-28} sts.

Size XS/S Only

Row 45 (Decrease Row – RS): Ch 1, turn, sk first st, sc in each st to last 4 sts, sc2tog, sk next st, sc in last st – 14 sts.

Row 46 (Decrease Row): Ch 3 (counts as dc), turn, dc2tog, dc in each st to end of row – 13 sts. Proceed to Shape Left Neck instructions.

Size M/L Only

Row 45 (Decrease Row – RS): Ch 1, turn, sk first st, sc in each st to last 4 sts, sc2tog, sk next st, sc in last st – 20 sts.

Row 46 (Decrease Row): Ch 3 (counts as dc), turn, dc2tog, dc in each st to last 3 sts, dc2tog, dc in last st – 18 sts.

Row 47 (Decrease Row): Ch 1, turn, sk first st, sc in each st to last 3 sts, sc2tog, sc in last st – 16 sts.

Row 48 (Decrease Row): Ch 3 (counts as dc), turn, dc2tog, dc in each st to end of row – 15 sts. Proceed to Shape Left Neck instructions.

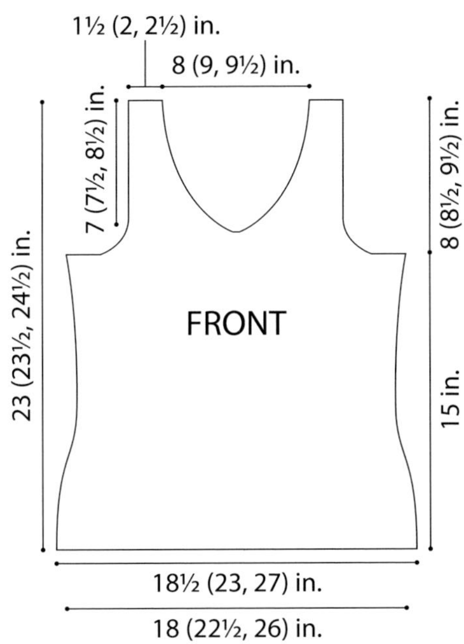

Size 1X/3X Only

Row 45 (Decrease Row – RS): Ch 1, turn, sk first st, sc in each st to last 3 sts, sc2tog, sc in last st – 26 sts.

Row 46 (Decrease Row): Ch 3 (counts as dc), turn, dc2tog, dc in each st to last 3 sts, dc2tog, dc in last st – 24 sts.

Rows 47 and 48: Rep Rows 45 and 46 – 20 sts.

Row 49: Rep Row 45 – 18 sts.

Row 50 (Decrease Row): Ch 3 (counts as dc), turn, dc2tog, dc in each st to end of row – 17 sts. Proceed to Shape Left Neck instructions.

Shape Left Neck

Row 1 (Decrease Row – RS): Ch 1, turn, sc in each st to last 4 sts, sc2tog, sk next st, sc in last st – 11{13-15} sts.

Row 2 (Decrease Row): Ch 3 (counts as dc), turn, dc2tog, dc in each st to end of row – 10{12-14} sts.

Row 3 (Decrease Row): Ch 1, turn, sc in each st to last 2 sts, sk next st, sc in last st – 9{11-13} sts.

Rows 4-7: Rep Rows 2 and 3 twice – 5{7-9} sts.

Row 8: Ch 3 (counts as dc), turn, dc in each st to end of row.

Row 9: Ch 1, turn, sc in each st to end of row.

Rows 10-13: Rep Rows 8 and 9 twice.

Row 14: Rep Row 8.

Shape Right Shoulder

Row 43 (RS): From RS, sk first 3 unworked sts following Row 43 of left shoulder, join yarn with a sc in next st, sc2tog, sc in each st to last 3 sts, sk next st, sc2tog – 19{25-30} sts.

Row 44 (Decrease Row): Ch 3 (counts as dc), turn, dc2tog, dc in each st to last 3 sts, dc2tog, dc in last st – 17{23-28} sts.

Size XS/S Only

Row 45 (Decrease Row): Ch 1, turn, sk first st, sc2tog, sc in each st to last 2 sts, sk next st, sc in last st – 14 sts.

Row 46 (Decrease Row): Ch 3 (counts as dc), turn, dc in each st to last 3 sts, dc2tog, dc in last st – 13 sts. Proceed to Shape Right Neck instructions.

Size M/L Only

Row 45 (Decrease Row): Ch 1, turn, sk first st, sc2tog, sc in each st to last 2 sts, sk next st, sc in last st – 20 sts.

Row 46 (Decrease Row): Ch 3 (counts as dc), turn, dc2tog, dc in each st to last 3 sts, dc2tog, dc in last st – 18 sts.

Row 47 (Decrease Row): Ch 1, turn, sk first st, sc in each st to last 2 sts, sk next st, sc in last st – 16 sts.

Row 48 (Decrease Row): Ch 3 (counts as dc), turn, dc in each st to last 3 sts, dc2tog, dc in last st – 15 sts. Proceed to Shape Right Neck instructions.

Size 1X/3X Only

Row 45 (Decrease Row): Ch 1, turn, sk first st, sc in each st to last 2 sts, sk next st, sc in last st – 26 sts.

Row 46 (Decrease Row): Ch 3 (counts as dc), turn, dc2tog, dc in each st to last 3 sts, dc2tog, dc in last st – 24 sts.

Rows 47 and 48: Rep Rows 45 and 46 – 20 sts.

Row 49: Rep Row 45 – 18 sts.

Row 50 (Decrease Row): Ch 3 (counts as dc), turn, dc in each st to last 3 sts, dc2tog, dc in last st – 17 sts. Proceed to Shape Right Neck instructions.

Shape Right Neck

Row 1 (Decrease Row – RS): Ch 1, turn, sk first st, sc2tog, sc in each st to end of row – 11{13-15} sts.

Row 2 (Decrease Row): Ch 3 (counts as dc), turn, dc in each st to last 3 sts, dc2tog, dc in last st – 10{12-14} sts.

Row 3 (Decrease Row): Ch 1, turn, sk first st, sc in each st to end of row – 9{11-13} sts.

Rows 4-7: Rep Rows 2 and 3 twice – 5{7-9} sts.

Row 8: Ch 3 (counts as dc), turn, dc in each st to end of row.

Row 9: Ch 1, turn, sc in each st to end of row.

Rows 10-13: Rep Rows 8 and 9 twice.

Row 14: Rep Row 8.
Fasten off.

FINISHING

From WS, sew or sl st shoulder seams. Sew or sl st side seams, leaving about 2" (5 cm) above lower edges unsewn to make side slits.

Armhole Edging

Rnd 1 (RS): From RS, join yarn with sl st in one armhole edge at underarm, ch 1, work an even number of sc evenly spaced around armhole edge; join with sl st in first sc.

Rnd 2 (WS): Ch 4 (counts as dc, ch 1), turn, sk first 2 sts, dc in next st, *ch 1, sk next st, dc in next st; rep from * to last st, ch 1, sk last st; join with sl st in 3rd ch of beg ch-4.
Fasten off.

Rep edging around 2nd armhole edge.

Neck Edging

Rnd 1 (RS): From RS, join yarn with sl st in neck edge at left shoulder seam so that you are ready to work along front neck edge, ch 1, work 61{65-73} sc evenly spaced along front neck edge to right shoulder seam, then work 37{39-41} sc evenly spaced along back neck edge to end of rnd; join with sl st in first sc – 98{104-114} sc.
Place a marker in the center sc of front neck edge.

Rnd 2 (WS): Ch 4, turn, sk first st (st immediately following same st as joining sl st was worked), dc in next st, *ch 1, sk next st, dc in next st; rep from * to 1 st before marked center front st, ch 1, sk next 3 sts, dc in next st, **ch 1, sk next st, dc in next st; rep from ** around, ch 1; join with sl st in 3rd ch of beg ch-4.
Fasten off.

Fringe

For each fringe, cut 3 strands of yarn about 14" (35.5 cm) long. Hold strands together and fold in half. With crochet hook, draw fold through a ch-1 sp along lower edge of Top, forming a loop. Pull ends of fringe through this loop and pull to tighten. Make a fringe in each ch-1 sp around lower edge of Front and Back.
Trim fringe ends evenly.

Each attached fringe will measure about 6" (15 cm) long.

If desired, trim every other fringe to about 4" (10 cm) long.

Weave in ends.

general Instructions

ABBREVIATIONS

beg = begin(ning)(s)
ch = chain
ch-sp(s) = chain space(s) previously made
cm = centimeters
dc = double crochet
hdc = half double crochet
mm = millimeters
rem = remain(ing)(s)
rep(s) = repeat(s)
RS = right side
rnd(s) = round(s)
sc = single crochet
sk = skip
sl st = slip stitch
sp(s) = space(s)
st(s) = stitch(es)
tog = together
WS = wrong side

* — When you see an asterisk used within a pattern row, the symbol indicates that later you will be told to repeat a portion of the instruction. Most often the instructions will say, repeat from * so many times.

( ) or **[ ]** — Sets off a short number of stitches that are repeated or indicates additional information.

– When you see – (dash) followed by a number of stitches, this tells you how many stitches you will have at the end of a row or round.

GAUGE

Never underestimate the importance of gauge. Achieving the correct gauge assures that the finished size of your piece matches the finished size given in the pattern.

CHECKING YOUR GAUGE

Work a swatch that is at least 4" (10 cm) square. Use the suggested hook size and the number of stitches given. If your swatch is larger than 4" (10 cm), you need to work it again using a smaller hook; if it is smaller than 4" (10 cm), try it with a larger hook. This might require a swatch or two to get the exact gauge given in the pattern.

METRICS

As a handy reference, keep in mind that 1 ounce = approximately 28 grams and 1" = 2.5 centimeters.

CROCHET TERMINOLOGY		
UNITED STATES		INTERNATIONAL
slip stitch (slip st)	=	single crochet (sc)
single crochet (sc)	=	double crochet (dc)
half double crochet (hdc)	=	half treble crochet (htr)
double crochet (dc)	=	treble crochet (tr)
treble crochet (tr)	=	double treble crochet (dtr)
double treble crochet (dtr)	=	triple treble crochet (ttr)
triple treble crochet (tr tr)	=	quadruple treble crochet (qtr)
skip	=	miss

TERMS

fasten off — To end your piece, you need to simply cut and pull the yarn through the last loop left on the hook. This keeps the last stitch intact and prevents the work from unraveling.

right side — Refers to the front of the piece.

BEGINNER	Projects for first-time crocheters using basic stitches. Minimal shaping.
EASY	Projects using yarn with basic stitches, repetitive stitch patterns, simple color changes, and simple shaping and finishing.
INTERMEDIATE	Projects using a variety of techniques, such as basic lace patterns or color patterns, mid-level shaping and finishing.
EXPERIENCED	Projects with intricate stitch patterns, techniques and dimension, such as non-repeating patterns, multi-color techniques, fine threads, small hooks, detailed shaping and refined finishing.

Yarn Weight Symbol & Names	LACE 0	SUPER FINE 1	FINE 2	LIGHT 3	MEDIUM 4	BULKY 5	SUPER BULKY 6	JUMBO 7
Type of Yarns in Category	Fingering, size 10 crochet thread	Sock, Fingering, Baby	Sport, Baby	DK, Light Worsted	Worsted, Afghan, Aran	Chunky, Craft, Rug	Super Bulky, Roving	Jumbo, Roving
Crochet Gauge* Ranges in Single Crochet to 4" (10 cm)	32-42 sts**	21-32 sts	16-20 sts	12-17 sts	11-14 sts	8-11 sts	6-9 sts	5 sts and fewer
Advised Hook Size Range	Steel*** 6 to 8, Regular hook B-1	B-1 to E-4	E-4 to 7	7 to I-9	I-9 to K-10½	K-10½ to M/N-13	M/N-13 to Q	Q and larger

*GUIDELINES ONLY: The chart above reflects the most commonly used gauges and hook sizes for specific yarn categories.

** Lace weight yarns are usually crocheted with larger hooks to create lacy openwork patterns. Accordingly, a gauge range is difficult to determine. Always follow the gauge stated in your pattern.

*** Steel crochet hooks are sized differently from regular hooks–the higher the number, the smaller the hook, which is the reverse of regular hook sizing.

CROCHET HOOKS	
U.S.	**Metric mm**
B-1	2.25
C-2	2.75
D-3	3.25
E-4	3.5
F-5	3.75
G-6	4
7	4.5
H-8	5
I-9	5.5
J-10	6
K-10½	6.5
L-11	8
M/N-13	9
N/P-15	10
P/Q	15
Q	16
S	19

LION BRAND® 24/7 COTTON®

Article #761

Weight Category: 4 - Medium Weight: Fashion garments, home décor, bath and kitchen accessories, and items for babies and children

Solids: 3.5oz/100g (186yd/170m)

Fiber Content: 100% Mercerized Cotton

Gauge:

Knit: 20 sts x 28 rows = 4 inches on size 6 [4 mm] needles

Crochet: 14 sc x 19 rows = 4 inches on G-6 [4 mm] hook

Product Care Instructions: Machine wash and dry.

VISIT LionBrand.com FOR:

- Learn to Knit & Crochet Instructions
- Weekly newsletter with articles, tips, and updates
- Store Locator

 Made in U.S.A.